A Pony Named Pickles

By Dr. Molly Tipton

Illustrated by Haley Jones

A Pony Named Pickles

Written by Dr. Molly Tipton

Illustrated by Haley Jones

The author and illustrator will always try to accommodate a book reading, speaking to a group, or appearing for a book signing or an interview. For more information or to book an event, contact Molly Tipton at:
Email: mollytiptonbooks@gmail.com
Instagram: @aponynamedpickles
Facebook: A Pony Named Pickles

To purchase autographed copies of this book, or for more information about the book, the author or the illustrator:

www.OklahomaBooksOnline.com/Pony_Named_Pickles

Publishing and Printing
by Total Publishing and Media (Tulsa, Okla.)

This edition printed in 2021.

ISBN 978-1-63302-186-0

TOTAL
PUBLISHING
&MEDIA

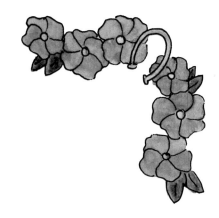

Acknowledgements

Thank you to Meredith for recognizing Pickle's need
for a home and my husband and
father for supporting both myself and my mother in
all our equine adventures. Most of all, I
recognize my mother for passing on a smidgeon of
her creativity to me, teaching me that all ponies need
love and that little girls never outgrow their pony.

This book is dedicated to Hunky, Camelot,
Josephine, Sooner, Raisin, Tee, Taz,
Albert, LuLu and to all the ponies.

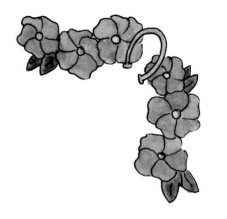

Ode to a Pickle

Sweet gherkins and dill can be

bought in the store.

There's just one pickle I love more.

You can have pickled okra.

You can buy pickled eggs.

But none are as loved;

As the pickle with legs.

Pickles was a pony in a small little square with
mud and leaves all tangled in his hair.

He was raggedy and skinny but the dirty,
brown pony had a cute little whinny.

Oh! How Pickles wished it would stop pouring.
He wished very hard the sun would come up this morning.

The rain itself was not too bad...
but the thunder made him pretty sad.

Pickles closed his eyes and thought real hard about living in a larger and greener yard.

He spent most of his time daydreaming so he would not get sad. His make-believe world was never bad.

He would dream about running
with wild mustangs and pawing the earth,
about lush green pastures and flowery turf.

Pickles was not scared.
He was a tough pony.
He was stuck outside alone though,
so he did get lonely.

It was a new day and the sun was bright.
He had just eaten a snack and was saving the rest for that night.

He had sunshine on his back and the
rain had stopped. He could just picture
himself grazing on a hilltop.

Flowers danced all around.
In his make-believe world, the stream even trickled
making a lovely sound.

After an afternoon nap and few strolls around his pen;
Pickles walked over to his food pan.

He was about to eat the last of his snack
when he heard a truck rumbling down the road out back.

To Pickles surprise, it turned into the drive!
It was a tall white truck pulling a small horse trailer.

A lady then stepped out
of the truck.
She stepped over a puddle
and around the muck.

She walked to the
trailer and opened
the door.
If only he were
taller; he could see
so much more!

Pickles tried to get up
on his toes;
but all he could see was
the trailer door close.

Pickles walked over to the corner of his pen.
He leaned up against the rusty tin.

He stood real tall and puffed out his chest.
He tried to look his very best.

That's when she started walking his way.
He was so shocked he let out a little
"NEIGH!"

Could this be it? Had the day come at last?
When this rusty pen would become his past?!

Pickles had been hopeful before,
only to be left out in the cold some more.

She opened the gate and grabbed a rope.
Was he good enough? He could only hope!

Oh! How handsome! The girl exclaimed.
But you look so sad and you've got tangles in your mane!

Have you had anything to eat at all?
You can come with me and
you'll have grass that is tall.

There is plenty of food and a cozy barn too
and I'll be there to love you.

She got really close and reached out her hand.
I heard you needed a home; a place with a friend.

Pickles was facing the
open trailer door.
He had been scared before
but not anymore.

With one last look at
his muddy pen
he turned his head
and hopped on in.

The trailer went down the road.
It creaked and bounced with its small load.

He stumbled only once then heard the girl say,
"We are here Pickles; a home where you can stay."

With a deep breath and his head held high;
he walked out to see where they had arrived.

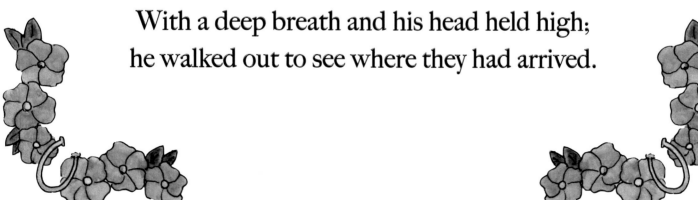

Oh! The flowers and
all the green grass,
a blue pond as clear as glass!

Pickles imagined
just what a thrill
it would be to
gallop over those hills.

He walked in the paddock
and the gate was closed.
He'd never felt so free or so

LOVED.

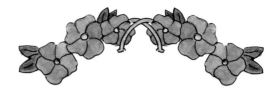

He closed his eyes
and thought about his
favorite daydream.
The one where he has a girl
and she loves him.

He lifted his nose,
a tear trickling down his face.
He had finally gotten
to that place!

He'd never known love
but knew without a doubt;
this was what it was all about.

Pickles before and
after his rescue.

Dr. Molly Tipton is an optometrist from rural
Alabama. She lives with her husband and dogs on
their farm where she enjoys caring for her horses and
ponies; including Pickles! Pickles was the first of
several rescued herd members that all live happily
ever after at their forever home on the farm.